# THE LEADERSHIP LEAP

# THE LEADERSHIP LEAP

*Transforming Managers into Visionaries*

MAXWELL STONEBRIDGE

QuantumQuill Press

# CONTENTS

| | | |
|---|---|---|
| 1 | Introduction | 1 |
| 2 | The Importance of Leadership | 3 |
| 3 | Developing Visionary Thinking | 5 |
| 4 | Building Strong Teams | 7 |
| 5 | Effective Communication Strategies | 9 |
| 6 | Inspiring and Motivating Others | 11 |
| 7 | Leading Through Change | 13 |
| 8 | Decision Making and Problem Solving | 15 |
| 9 | Emotional Intelligence and Empathy | 17 |
| 10 | Ethical Leadership | 19 |
| 11 | Cultivating Innovation and Creativity | 21 |
| 12 | Coaching and Mentoring | 23 |
| 13 | Balancing Work and Life | 25 |
| 14 | Continuous Learning and Personal Growth | 27 |
| 15 | Conclusion | 29 |

Copyright © 2024 by Maxwell Stonebridge

All rights reserved. No part of this book may be reproduced in any manner whatsoever without written permission except in the case of brief quotations embodied in critical articles and reviews.

First Printing, 2024

# CHAPTER 1

# Introduction

The Leadership Leap is unique in its structure, guiding readers from a traditional path of management and opens their mind in each chapter to becoming a more effective leader. Leaders can no longer be all-knowing, omnipotent figures who have all the answers. The scale, complexity, pace, and uncertainty we work in gives everyone a hard time. Today's job is to create a system with the capacity to adapt. Leaders must develop the talents of their teams to ensure each of them can deal with new challenges and develop effective solutions. Starting today, create space for your team to succeed and develop their talents; build approaches that can cope with the rapid, unpredictable changes coming your way. Arenas, to keep up and adapt to the changes that have never been seen before.

Challenging economic times are demanding a new vision for leadership, essential for organizational success and a vibrant financial future. The Leadership Leap shares the secrets of successful leaders, enabling reluctant managers to become truly visionary leaders. Today's leading contributors and leadership experts offer their invaluable insights, experience, and guidance, including Mike Abrashoff, Lt. Gen. Bernard Banks, Albert "Skip" Church, Col. Art Athens,

Col. Dick Merrin, Dr. Bruce L. Rhoades, Dr. Linda Sharkey, Dr. Justin Menkes, Morris Graham, Jr., Dr. Alan Maryon-Davis, Tasha Eurich, Troy Waugh, Christopher Novak, Col. Corey New, Terence Mauri, Madelyn E. Blair along with Editor, Natasha Simmons.

# CHAPTER 2

# The Importance of Leadership

Sher led an initiative in 2007 to reorganize CyberCraft's processes, rebuilding a slimmed-down infrastructure in a way that recognized the company's rapid growth - a doubling of business from 2006 to 2007, with another doubling already underway by mid-2008. "We started from scratch to develop a new process that emphasizes simplicity and focuses on our customers - our independent engineers," says Sher. Under the new process, CyberCraft now has "no more than seven layers [of governance]," he says. "The new process makes it faster to implement simplicity, and therefore easier for engineers to provide the products and deliver the quality that make our customers happy." CyberCraft's new process is not only less bureaucratic, it promotes additional leadership throughout the organization. By decentralizing decision making, an array of employees are empowered to act. Leaderless teams built around knowledge and expertise, rather than rank and title, have become the basis of a new management structure at CyberCraft.

CyberCraft has built its business on the notion that well-tested processes are the key to developing high-quality custom software. But in 2007, the company's internal processes - the ones it used to manage its base of 5,000 independent test engineers in 90 countries - became so complex and bloated with overhead that the business was threatened. Eran Sher, program manager at CyberCraft, recalls how the obstacles a slow-moving corporate bureaucracy were creating could not be overcome within the company's existing business model. The process that fostered its marketplace of independent test engineers required a lighter, more responsive touch.

**CHAPTER 3**

# Developing Visionary Thinking

You can be visionary with the same data that is available to all or any of us. You just need an interior perception powers, ignite your interior brain processes, then begin to share your thoughts in a way that others. It is not necessary to be acknowledged by others to begin engaging in leadership into the future. It is also not necessary to wait until you are granted a title or status that is usually assigned to those we assume lead and direct it. While those who make the future possible will, within any hierarchy, have the formal role of leader, the bottoms of the pyramid will vary the position of the game when they get into the discussion about what is possible. Once you recognized, as so many front line employees of leader companies do, that you, too, are a head (a person with the capability to influence others to grasp a vision of what is important), you are on your way not only to being aware about a much broader landscape, but also to making it so.

Each one of us has the capability to be visionary. Quite simply, leaders have the capacity to use visionary thinking creatively.

Therefore, envisioning the future is not reserved for inventors or scientists who come up with the brand new (although we certainly would love more of these people). Using data for the world as we now know it, we have available to us to imagine a future that could be different is not the reserve of senior executives. The market leaders we admire in research or in the various domain names where frontiers are being signed up with are not using a special mental template that only a few have. Critics have vision, activists have vision, front-line employees have very clear and compelling visions. You do not have to reserve a chair at the top of the org chart to get in touch with the parts of others that will develop a more advanced society. Once again, we have such a great deal of evidence because there are many examples of people without any surnames who have made such excellent changes in our life.

# CHAPTER 4

# Building Strong Teams

Leaders employ the LEAP model. It begins with the structure of the team. It is important for the leader to make certain that each member is invested with the accountability to contribute to the team's success. Each member must be attentive to both results and the quality and quantity of work required to achieve established goals. Discussions will resonate, first with what has been accomplished and then with planned initiatives. The LEAP model reminds us that A-for-Alignment is equally crucial in building a strong team. Each member must be dedicated in both thought and action to corporate objectives. This requires commitment and the subordination of personal concerns, if necessary, to ensure that progress is unimpeded. After all, leaders recognize that coherence, consistency, and dependability on the part of team members are essential to moving the organization forward.

Great leaders build great teams. This is no simple task. It's estimable, but it is also the key to transforming a good organization into a great one. Successful leaders accept the adage "hire for attitude/train for skill." They desire passion every bit as much as they demand experience. Those who lead successful organizations are those who bring together teams in which members mutually elevate productivity, morale, and innovation. Leaders believe that teams, in essence, are more than the sum of their parts. They also believe that great teams can be built in a unique way. I refer to the LEAP model which leads to the development of strong teams.

# CHAPTER 5

# Effective Communication Strategies

As a leader, it is important to use the appropriate mode of communications to disseminate information. The traditional mode of communication, as mentioned earlier, has been confined to meetings, notice boards, and verbal communication. However, today's mode includes newsletters, e-mails, and a host of web-based communications platforms such as Twitter, LinkedIn, blogs, etc. Knowing that communication encompasses more than speaking and writing, successful leaders have to take into account body language. The ability to communicate empathetically improves the quality of relationships and the ability to bridge the gap between the leader and followers. Leaders who communicate with empathy are "adept at deliberately constructing messages that communicate an understanding of how others think and feel, and then communicate that understanding to others". To improve empathy, it is important to listen actively to others with open-mindedness, avoid bias and favoritism, and acknowledge emotions of others.

Most traditional leaders in the workplace have been encouraged to work in silos since the organizational structure of most companies is vertical and not horizontal. It has been the norm for leaders to be seen and not heard unless directing or criticizing. With the advancement in the way organizations work and the future of the workplace, known to be supported by technology, it is imperative that leaders change to be more futuristic and communicative. The way leaders communicate is invaluable in reaching out to employees and managing change. Most importantly, the company shares information that allows employees to feel valued, allows them to have positive psychological ownership, and hence manage change effectively. Studies have shown that leaders are empathetic and often articulate their purpose more effectively.

# CHAPTER 6

# Inspiring and Motivating Others

You earn trust by being credible and consistent, by telling people the truth. People quite easily see through flawed reasoning and inconsistency. They also easily pick up insincerity. Telling the truth, keeping promises, maintaining consistency between word and its acts make someone credible. People are not an exception. They reward those who do so, that's what makes someone a trustworthy leader. Credible leaders are also consistent. They don't change opinions according to the latest poll or the desires of those around them. They earn their leadership, rather than expecting it as a right. Those who trust others also trust themselves – they believe they are able to distinguish those who are trustworthy from those who aren't. Such trust is not only the foundation to create credibility; it is also an expression by the top management—a very explicit one—of their willingness to accept risk.

You'll need to win the trust of the people you're leading. Trust can't be forced or taken by anyone in a position of authority. You can't manipulate people into trusting you by "putting a lot of effort into it". The more you declare that you must be trusted because you're the boss or "a person in authority", the less credible you are. There are deep roots for mistrusting management, so it's naïve – if not largely arrogant – to assume that people should trust someone by the simple fact of their being in authority. Trust, like inspiration and fellowship, is earned. Trust also entails risk. It can't be given in advance to top management or to anyone who's in a management position, because there's always a probabilistic risk. Risk—no matter how well calculated—means the likelihood of things turning out differently from what was expected, and consequences that no endorsement can avoid or cancel. So, unfortunately, things don't quite work this way: "We're the boss, trust us."

# CHAPTER 7

# Leading Through Change

The five actions within the leading through change dimension are the best practices of leaders who are able to successfully bridge the gap between leading individuals and leading teams, are able to show their values and stand by them (even when it is uncomfortable), and are able to create a vision for the future that they can share. Change is the process that is required to make the first four happen; it is the impact area of our framework where we make it all happen. Managers fail because they fail to change themselves and their behaviors; they fail to see how they can leverage others to impact change. You cannot lead others until you first lead yourself and begin to change. Leaders know that change must happen until their team can be purposeful and effective. They must be communicating this need continuously. It is also about leading change, carving a path through that is not self-sabotaging. Leadership cannot be negative and manipulative. It requires courage, strength, and wisdom when executing change.

A leader who can imagine a future and who can share that vision with their team provides a powerful force for change. When building the power of their leadership, we focus on the vision, values, and team dimensions shown in the diagram above. If leaders were only leading individuals, these would be the only three. However, leaders bring about change too. When they first step into their role, this change often feels more like damaging existing relationships. After all, when individuals become promoted into their first management position, the people that once were their peers are now under their control. We focus on the leadership dimensions: relationships, team, values, and change because it is here that the new, purposeful leader will make the "Leadership Leap".

## CHAPTER 8

# Decision Making and Problem Solving

Results desired are not problem sets; they are goals, objectives, and purposes. It is one thing if decision-making processes fail at the organizational level; it is another if the man in charge is inept at making decisions that deter the organization and those around him from acting in the organizational interest. They are often forced to operate strictly in self-interest to avoid the uncertainty that comes with the previous poor decision-making processes. Recognition and organization go hand in hand, especially with regards to making decisions and solving problems. The authoritative and decisive manager, as opposed to those who pose conflicting processes and timid personalities, is able to project an image and credibility that is comforting to those who are looking to be led and the organization by which he is charged. The leader understands the significance of their organization's people and the problem that arises when the mismanagement of them becomes masked by the forces of globalization; that is why timely organization rewards provide that competitive advantage.

It is common for organizations to make decisions quickly and inefficiently, then blame the outcome on poor leadership, the economy, bad luck or any number of reasons that validate the negative consequences of acting with limited information and often blatant disregard for foreseeable consequences. They find themselves in this predicament because their problems are always analyzed as they presented themselves in the past instead of the problem in its present state, which is compounded by the manager's inability to be truly decisive. The solution to these managers' problems is relatively simple: the decision-making process and the problems that resulted from it were never based on what the manager thought were truly important in relation to the preferred outlook of what the outcome would be once the decisions were made.

# CHAPTER 9

# Emotional Intelligence and Empathy

Furthermore, she underscored the importance of empathy in successful leadership. In the "Harvard Business Review," author Annie McKee described empathy as the "purest and highest form of emotional intelligence," defining it as "not only understanding others but caring about their feelings and concerns." McKee asserted that empathy transforms a good leader into a "great leader" and said it was powerful enough to alleviate a suffering employee from his/her stress or depression. Indeed, two studies from the Center for Creative Leadership concluded that empathy is an essential quality which makes a leader both effective and respected, further pointing out that empathy is also paramount to gaining employee trust.

Anne Tyson, regional career manager for Lee Hecht Harrison, a talent solutions company, wrote an incisive article about emotional intelligence and its impact on leadership. She said the term "emotional intelligence" was first coined by authors Peter Salavoy and John Mayer, before Daniel Goldman wrote the 1995 best-seller, "Emotional Intelligence." In 2017, Travis Bradbury and Jean Graves penned the book, "Emotional Intelligence 2.0," which explored how the most renowned leaders in business were strong in areas such as self-awareness and management, social awareness, relationship management, personal effectiveness, and work-life balance. All these aspects of emotional intelligence, Tyson said, describe what is known as a "great boss and team leader."

# CHAPTER 10

# Ethical Leadership

The framework contributes to an understanding of the transformative process from "managers" to "leaders", as well as from the development of vision to the realization of vision, through understanding the universal dimension of the personal values that drive vision, ethical behavior, and leadership. In this perspective, ethical leadership is seen not only as a foundation and a fundamental propellant for vision realization but also as the beacon for responsible and purposeful leadership. Scholars and practitioners agree that ethical leadership is a cornerstone of effective leadership in the long run. There are two fundamental, almost self-evident ethical tasks for leaders: the formulation and realization of ethical vision.

Without going into the details of the global failures on the part of major financial, business, and political institutions that the world has witnessed in recent years, it is increasingly evident that there is a crying need for a new paradigm of leadership and management that is both effective and sustainable in the longer term. In this context, no theory or set of principles about leadership that ignore ethics in general, and ethical leadership in particular, can ever hope to be taken seriously. This chapter deals with the evident value of integrating this concept into a holistic framework of leadership.

# CHAPTER 11

# Cultivating Innovation and Creativity

While incumbents cull through outmoded strategic tactic options that no longer apply, new and innovative entrants to the market redefine customer experiences or operating models with creative and innovative methods that challenge orthodoxy. Being creative means being audacious, radical, and audacious. Innovators, then, look for ideas everywhere through tapping into so-called adjacent potential and simultaneously using what they already know to be true as a springboard. Leaders of institutions, in particular, must be open to converting the new insights they receive into game-changing business models. None of this is new, of course; such narrative is full of truisms from people like our modern-day Technophiles and others less celebrated or popular, and dated social, political, and economic events that rely on innovation and creativity emerge as the underlying drivers of transformation. They are the unambiguous choices needed for their followers to achieve superior performance – not when things are easy.

Enterprises of the future must find a way to convert cutting-edge visions into successful business models. Only then can an organization compete for the hearts, minds, and wallets of its clients, who, thanks to digital technology, are savvier than ever about a product, brand, and company's proposition. The key for the Digital Advocate is to balance today's business with the technology and operations transformations that are themselves inherently difficult, but singularly address the need to operate by a new set of rules. Stuck in the middle of doing both things, they need tools, frameworks, and support structures. They need to either reinvent their leadership style to address this duality or have the mindset to prepare to be replaced by new visionary leaders of their organizations who have this new leadership design built into their DNA.

# CHAPTER 12

# Coaching and Mentoring

Individual concerns should be addressed in processes which will "tend to business." Employees should be made aware, in a way that their confidentiality is protected, that they do not have to leave individual or health problems of a family nature at home; that work-family interface problems are all part of the human condition. Notice if there is a long-term corporate environment problem (like a lack of child care) that impacts many. If the situational problem is more corporate than personal, the boss should intercede and take the query to higher levels in the organization. Remember, it's much easier to meet a problem head on than to run and hide from it.

One of the most important skills a leader should have is knowing how to deal with employees in various ways and levels. Delegating is a fine art. The most important principle to remember is that, with any task assigned, make certain that the delegated responsibility is paralleled with the necessary authoritative responsibility, empowerment, and creative freedom so those endeavoring to succeed have the power needed to give direction. A leader must have faith in another's potential, lest the person's self-confidence be lost; while at the same time, the person should be held accountable for achieving the task.

Employees need to understand that "eyes" are watching them and, just like children, are better behaved and work harder when they realize "father watches." In addition, when work is done well, be sure to show your sincere appreciation.

# CHAPTER 13

# Balancing Work and Life

One year, an organization might have to manage all of these project managers or a group of managers to broaden itself out so that everyone can have a clear career path no matter what. Such an allocation is especially important for institutions in kind communities in which project managers are regularly flung out into new surroundings. Then releases for middle management may be able to start with more information and support, but they can also ensure that the job and profession of project managers are not jeopardized after retirement. Additionally, keep asking while you review, "Is it feasible or necessary to transfer the job back so that the job is not overheated throughout our project life?" In relation to promoting mid-level management into the most successful position at the right time.

Being an effective project manager often depends on spending time in a new or unfamiliar field, and you will need time to study when you get there. Balancing that intense time with family, leisure, and self-care is important but also quite difficult. In addition, the small moments of freedom between the intense weeks of the project manager may not turn into something at all, but feeling confident in your own progress may assist in continuing to handle a large workload and learning what you need to do in order to adjust those little spots of time eventually.

Talented leadership is always in demand and perpetually in short supply. For certain companies, managers will become overwhelmed. We have a constant assumption, especially in the United States, that the most talented, most organized, and most helpful professional has the greatest workload. We have only approximately eight or nine hours of willpower per day. Learn about the signs and avoid burnout.

# CHAPTER 14

# Continuous Learning and Personal Growth

Most means of personal development or change are focused on effecting change - "changing oneself." In order for us to progress on the path of continuous learning and personal growth so that we better ourselves becomes the constant objective. The road on the journey of continuous learning and personal development that big-time leaders pursue is essential for they themselves to lead and inspire the entire organization. Arthur A. Naiman, in his book The Leadership Leap: A Big Time Leader, has effectively narrated this triad of continuous learning, personal growth and leadership. Here are thoughts from the book that could help you to grow - both personally and as a leader and visionary. These thoughts encompass the growth journey of leaders, make stale layers of complacency peel off and stimulate personal and professional progress.

As Peter Drucker predicted last century, the 21st century is shaping up as the century of unparalleled change and opportunity. The dislocations and transformations we have already seen, not to mention those ahead, require a change and transformation in the nature of leadership. To fill this void, Arthur A. Naiman presents a philosophy and a program he calls "The Big Time Leader" - an impressive concept that "fills the leadership vacuum" and that will prepare future leaders to meet the changing challenges of society. The book is about the all-important "leap" from manager to visionary leader. It is a critical addition to literature on the subject of leadership and sets out a well-considered case for the author's unique beliefs that big-time leaders must (1) engage in continuous learning and personal growth, (2) help employees deliver "A" performance, (3) lead with "head and heart," (4) be optimists, and (5) develop vision, strategy, and plan.

# CHAPTER 15

# Conclusion

As this is not designed as an objective article, we leave many provocative conclusions unexplored and will progress towards an endeavor to establish esteemed attributes and cover the revolution with a comfortable title sounding abstract (and pretending to be synthetic), not dissimilar to a mission statement.

Byzantine hierarchies converge not only towards the heavenly empire but also towards voluminous committees and intricate power pedestals. But what is it that makes hermits and solitaires enjoy the same enigma as the profound Inquisitor? By firmly anchored postulates of apparent causation, psychological singularities independent of the 'chosen' struggle march to the absolute conflict over 'the great cause'. Each one subdivides ad infinitum in the hope of existence assurance and sings the demise of the universal whole.

We directed our attention to the fundamental and endemic human propensity for subsystems (or matrices) to find their justification in further subsystems. At a point sufficiently distant in the hierarchy or as a unitary entity itself, the concept or individual feels entitled to its own description and cultivation and to rely on the observed distinctions from a lesser occur only by the favor of the legitimacy-giving host. We rest our faith on organs and entities too distant to be understood and too intricate to fulfill the criterion of existence and being (like the hidden logos subsuming the dialogs).

In times of dramatic change and when the forces of transformation conspire to nullify the relevance of traditional models of leadership, why take a leap towards one which is known, in the end, by arrogant and naive attributes? Why does arrogance gain credence, and what fatality befalls the apolitical visionary?

Milton Keynes UK
Ingram Content Group UK Ltd.
UKHW040740301124
451843UK00010B/230